Table of Contents

Making it in Hollywood

Tinsel Town is a place for aspiring actors and actresses to grow. It is a chance for these youngsters to find where they belong, and make a name for themselves in the world of entertainment. Success in Hollywood, while often glorified, is not easily achieved. For those who do find success, the rewards are often great. It is only the fighters, and those who believe failure is a motivator, or a lesson from which to grow, that will reach stardom.

Marilyn Monroe once stated, "I used to think as I looked out on the Hollywood night, there must be a thousand girls sitting alone like me dreaming of being a movie star. But I'm not going to worry about them, I'm dreaming the hardest."(1) This says it all. There are going to be hundreds, if not thousands of people fighting like you to make it big, but you have to fight the hardest to push through the crowd and be the one to make it.

It takes a great deal of patience, perseverance, strategizing, and failure to make it. Each small success is oftentimes praised, as those opportunities, no matter how small, are the doors to bigger possibilities. Your career beginner is often unexpected, and you should walk through all doors to have the best chance. That being said, with fame comes responsibility. You are often seen as a model by society. You have to look a certain way, act a certain way, and keep your nose clean, all while carrying a lot of responsibilities on your shoulders. With that burden resting on your shoulder you still have to be yourself.

You are the key to making it. It is your personality, your actions, and your aspirations that people will believe in.

Like Jack Nicholson once stated; "I learned a long time ago in Hollywood that the only person I should vote for is myself."(2) This statement just speaks to the need of an aspiring actor or actress to push on, because there will be naysayers and failures that will push you down on your way to the top. If you believe in yourself and your abilities you will win.

For those who stood above the crowd and made it, congratulations for you are where you wanted to be. As stated earlier those who make it have to not only be true to themselves, but also hold up to the standards of society, as a role model for aspiring youngsters trying to make it. While expected to be perfect, the reality is that celebrities are human too, and humans make mistakes. Sometimes these mistakes can be an experience to learn from, and other times it can result in tragedy. Today you will embark on a journey that takes you through decades of celebrity mistakes that turned into public scandals. Are you ready for the ride?

Scandals and Mysteries 1900-1940

The Start of Hollywood

Hollywood wasn't the glorified "City of Stars" it is now. At its start the area now known as Hollywood was one hut centered in a desolate town named Nopalera. The land surrounding the hut was used for agricultural purposes. After the agricultural industry began to grow and more people moved to Nopalera, the city became an agricultural hub.

With the booming industry came a new name and the city's name was changed to Cahuenga Valley in 1870. It wasn't until Mr. Harvey Wilcox and his wife strode into town that the city started to develop into what is now Hollywood. The pair bought more than 160 acres of land in Cahuenga Valley, and with a city blueprint in hand they began to develop what later became known as "Tinsel Town."

As development began in the city so did an increase in the town's population. Due to the increase in the developing city, the town received the rights to build a post office, hotel, and school. During this time there was also a migration of filmmakers and actors from restrictive New Jersey to the land of opportunity. These individuals sought to make movies the way they wanted without strict guidelines controlling them, and California was just the right place to get started.

The first film made in California was shot during this time. The film was titled *In Old California*. With the help of Los Angeles, Hollywood welcomed its first film studio Nestor Company in 1911. After the creation of the studio, other motion-picture companies began migrating to the town, thus creating a perfect hub for filmmakers, actors, and entertainers to prosper.

With the development of Hollywood came actors and actresses looking to make a name for themselves. Entertainers like Mary Pickford, Fatty Arbuckle and Spencer Tracy were making their mark on the industry. With so much success, came social responsibility that not everyone welcomed or acknowledged. While business was booming, so were the scandals surrounding some of the most famous entertainers of their time.

Lover's Revenge: Evelyn Nesbit

Date: June 25th, 1906
Location: Rooftop Theater of Madison Square Garden
Victim: Stanford White
Defendant: Henry Kendal Thaw
Cause of Death: Gunshot to the Face

Evelyn Nesbit Back Story:

Evelyn Nesbit born Florence Evelyn Nesbit was born December 25th, 1884 to parents Winfried Scott Nesbit and Evelyn Florence Nesbit in Pittsburg, Pennsylvania. In her early life Nesbit flocked to her father. Her father supported her intellectually, which was unusual considering the male perspective on a female during those times. He fostered her intellect by building her a library filled with books they would often read together. He was supportive of everything she did, and when she wanted to take up singing and dancing her father encouraged her to take lessons.

The family moved to Pittsburg some years later in 1893. Her father died a few years later, which left the family in a financially unstable situation. They were forced out of their home and forced to live off the charity of family and friends. When Nesbit's mother scrounged up enough money, the two of them rented a home that she turned into a boarding house. Nesbit had changed from little girl to rent collector. After several years the business failed. Nesbit's mother went to Philadelphia in search of better moneymaking opportunities and left Evelyn and her brother with family.

When Nesbit's mother found success as a sales clerk at Wanamaker's, she moved her two children to Philadelphia and they worked alongside her. It was at this job that Nesbit was discovered. She became a model for a small group of talented artists in the area. Nesbit graced the cover of notable magazines such as Vanity Fair, Harper's Bazaar, and even Cosmopolitan. After a few years in the business it became a bore and she set her sights on Broadway. Her first role came in the play *Florodoro* at the Casino Theater. She played in the chorus. When the play ended Nesbit gained a featured role in the play *Wild Horse*.

It was around that time when Nesbit met Stanford White. He was a ladies' man and had his sights set on Nesbit. The pair were decades apart in age. A member of the play had introduced them and both were invited to his home. They shared lunch and a tour of the actor's home. He eventually moved Nesbit and her family into a suite at the Wellington Hotel. He began taking on the fatherly role in Nesbit's life, which comforted her mother. It comforted her so much so she was convinced that a trip out of town to visit her old friends in Pittsburg without the child was ok. It was during her mother's trip that things got a little tricky.

A few days into being home alone together the pair shared a meal and drinks, before going on another tour of White's home. He led her to this mirror of rooms that he had just added to the home. It was there where they shared a few more drinks. Nesbit maintains that at some point she passed out and when she woke up she was laying next to White naked. She was no longer a virgin.

A Turning Point:
Nesbit kept the incident hidden for many years, still allowing White to play the father figure in her life. A few

years later Nesbit met Henry Kendall Thaw. He was the son of a coal and railroad baron and heir to a $40 million inheritance. While at a showing of *Wild Horse*, in which Nesbit was featured, Thaw used false pretenses to set up a meeting with her. He explained to her his name was Mr. Monroe, but later came forward with his true Identity.

The pair began to see each other, and convinced her mother to come along with them on a trip to Europe. The trip was supposed to be relaxing as Nesbit had just come out of surgery and was still feeling the effects. A packed itinerary proved to be burdensome on Nesbit and she and her mother began to argue. Thaw and Nesbit went on to the next leg of the trip, leaving her mother behind. While on the trip Thaw asked Nesbit for her hand in marriage. She declined. She believed that because she was no longer a virgin, due to White's indecencies, she was tainted and unfit to marry. She maintains that unless she let go of her burden that she would not be able to accept the proposal. That's when she told Thaw of the events that took place years earlier. The two shared tears. Thaw had thoughts of getting even with White.

While on their European vacation, Thaw planned a stay in Castle SchlossKatzenstein. It was there that his rage, which he said was geared toward White, was taken out on Nesbit. She was subjected to beatings from Thaw for two weeks. At the end he apologized for his behavior and the two headed back to New York City where they were later married. Thaw never forgot what happened to Nesbit and made it his business to seek revenge. At one point in time he carried a gun because he thought White was having him followed.

The Night in Question:
Thaw and Nesbit, along with two of his friends made their way to the Rooftop Theater in Madison Square Garden. After several failed attempts Thaw approached White and shot him three times in the face, killing him instantly. His face was virtually unrecognizable. Thaw was said to have shouted, "I did it because you ruined my wife! He had it coming to him. He took advantage of the girl and abandoned her!"(3)

The Trial:
Thaw had two trials in which Nesbit was the star witness. It was said that the Thaw family had promised her money to say only positive things about her husband. The case was sensationalized in the media and it became the first time in US history that a jury had to be sequestered. The first trial started on January 23rd, 1907. After 47 hours of deliberation, the jury rendered a split decision. Seven jurors voted guilty, while five said not guilty. The ruling did not sit well with Thaw, as he was upset that the jury did not recognize the chivalry he had displayed in retaliating against a man that had taken away a woman's innocence. Thaw was tried again a year later. Thaw claimed temporary insanity and was sentenced to life in Matteawan State for the criminally insane.

Conclusion:
Thaw put together a legal team that helped him prove to a judge that he was now legally sane and ended up getting out of Matteawan State. Nesbit released two memoirs of her life.

The Rape and Manslaughter Trial of Fatty Arbuckle

Date: September 5th, 1921
Location: St. Francis Hotel, Room 1219
Victim: Virginia Rappe
Defendant: Actor Roscoe "Fatty" Arbuckle
The Evidence: Bruising on the body and a ruptured bladder

Arbuckle's Backstory

Fatty Arbuckle, born Roscoe Arbuckle was born March 24, 1887 to parents William Goodrich Arbuckle and Mollie Arbuckle. Weighing 13 pounds at birth, the comedian was named after a philandering politician in office during the time. At two years of age Arbuckle moved with his family to Santa Ana California. At age four he was gracing the stage of Frank Bacons Company.

It was known that the comedian had a great singing voice. At 12, the young entertainer was forced to pick up odd jobs, as his father would not support his entertaining career. While working, a customer noticed Arbuckle's voice and urged him to enter an amateur talent show. He showed the audience his talents, which, in turn, helped launch his career.

Arbuckle graced many stages in his vaudeville career with the first being a theater owned by Sam Grauman. He played at several other theaters and traveled with different vaudeville troupes to include Pantages Theatre Group, and Orpheum Theater. During his fame he was married three times.

After 1913 Arbuckle began his lucrative career as an on screen comedian obtaining a deal that would later earn him a 3 year $3 million dollar contract with Paramount Pictures. By 1916 the fame was getting to the comedian as he gained excessive weight and began to turn to alcohol for comfort. He was later to recover and start his own film company. His success was short lived though as the Scandal of 1921 rocked Hollywood.

On the Night in Question:
Arbuckle along with friends Lowell Sherman and Fred Fischbach drove to San Francisco. Arbuckle had earlier received an injury to his buttocks that resulted in second-degree burns. The trio took the trip as an escape from work, which had become frantic.

When the trio got to the St. Francis Hotel they checked into rooms 1219, 1220, and 1221. Two of the rooms were for private usage, while the other was to be used for a party venue in which they would later invite eligible women and friends to come and party with them.

During the party a young starlet by the name of Virginia Rappe was found in room 1219. She was examined by a medical doctor who confirmed that the ill stricken starlet was sick due to intoxication.

Victim's Condition at a Glance:
September 8th, 1921 Virginia Rappe had cystitis, which was known to flare up during periods of intoxication and could cause her body to experience immense pain. When Rappe visited the doctor three days after being examined at St. Francis Hotel her friend informed the presiding doctor that the star had been physically raped by "Fatty", though no signs of rape were found upon a doctor's examination. Rappe died just one day after visiting the

doctor in the hospital. The cause of death was noted as peritonitis, a condition that was brought on by a ruptured spleen.

Taking a Closer Look:
Although the doctor's examination turned up no evidence that suggested Arbuckle raped Rappe, reports surfaced that he did in fact commit the act. In fact, Virginia's friend who had earlier accompanied her to the doctor, made an accusation to the police claiming again that Arbuckle had raped Virginia Rappe.

Virginia's manager also made accusations against the comedian indicating his involvement in her death, though it was found out later that he could have been making such allegations to solicit monies from Arbuckle's attorneys. The police concluded that the force of Arbuckle's weight on top of the starlet's body aided in the rupture of her spleen, therefore causing her death.

Arbuckle's Account of Events:
Arbuckle maintained that he found Rappes in room 1219, as he was on his way to change clothes and head into town. When he found Rappe she was ill, and he carried her to the bed so she could rest. He then enlisted the help of other guests to help treat the starlet. He maintains after the doctor checked her out he left the room with another guest.

Taking it to Court:
The Arbuckle case was tried three times in court. During the trials witnesses testified to the character of Arbuckle. The media claimed the vaudeville comedian preyed on young girls, and sensationalized the case in periodicals.

The prosecutor assigned to the case was even said to have coerced witnesses into making false statements against Arbuckle.

The star witness in the case was Maude Delmont, Rappe's friend. It was later decided she should not take the stand because of her spotty history with the law, and constant preying on wealthy men. During the first trial Arbuckle was charged with manslaughter. Due to mishandling of the case by the prosecution, the jury came to a 10-2 decision and the case was declared a mistrial.

The second trial began on January 11th, 1922. The only players that had changed in the courtroom were the jury. The same evidence was heard and the same witnesses were called. During this trial witnesses came forward letting the court know they were coerced into making false statements to the court in the first trial, and some witnesses were discredited due to their criminal history. After several hours of deliberation the jury came to the same 10-2 decision as the first trial.

Arbuckle went to trial once more during the case in March of 1922. By this time the comedian's career was down the drain. His movies had been banned and reports of his story were circling around in the media. A verdict of not guilty was rendered within six minutes of jury deliberation. They also wrote and read a public apology to the defendant.

Case Conclusion:
Arbuckle was exonerated of the manslaughter charge against him. He did have to pay a $500 fine for having alcohol present at the party, which was a violation of the

Volstead Act. The comedian was also blacklisted in Hollywood, and left for broke due to the debt he accumulated during the three public trials.

The Death of William Desmond Taylor

Date: February 1st, 1922
Time: 8:00 P.M.
Location: Alvarado Court Apartment Homes, Los Angeles California
Victim: William Desmond Taylor
Suspects: Charlotte Shelby, Mabel Normand, Edward Sands, Charles Eyton, Henry Peavey, Faith Cole MacLean, Mary Miles Minter
Cause Of Death: Gunshot wound to the back

Desmond Taylor's Backstory:

William Desmond Taylor was born William Cunningham Deane-Tanner on April 26th, 1872. He was born to father Kearns Deane-Tanner and mother Jane Deane-Tanner in Carlow, Ireland. In December of 1912 Taylor had begun his career in Hollywood.

With a new name, William Desmond Taylor, in hand and success at the forefront of his mind Taylor landed several jobs at the start of his career. The most noted appearance was his three-time cameo alongside Margaret Gibson, a silent film actress. In 1914 William Desmond Taylor was directing his first film. The film was titled *The Awakening.*

While Taylor's success in Hollywood was plenty, making over 50 films, he found time to serve in the Canadian Expeditionary Force. As a private in the Force in 1918, he was assigned to the Royal Army Service Corps, before being promoted to the position of Lieutenant in January 1919. Before leaving the Force in April of that same year, Taylor had been promoted to Major.

After Taylor's move out of the Canadian Expeditionary Force, he returned to Hollywood. His return was much celebrated, as he was welcomed with an honorary banquet given to him by the Motion Picture Directors' Association. With so much celebration Taylor got right back in the saddle, directing some of the most popular films of the time. Taylor also had a few love interests. He was engaged to silent film actress Neva Gerber, though the two never married.

On the Night in Question:
February 1st, 1922 Taylor was said to be enjoying drinks with Mabel Normand at Alvarado Court Apartment Homes, Los Angeles California. At 7:45pm he was seen leaving his apartment with Mrs. Normand. The two walked to her car and bid each other a good night before she drove away.

At 8:00pm, after Taylor went back into his home, something sounding like a car backfire was heard by others living in the area. Neighbors maintained that they saw what looked to be a man dressed in a long coat and a cover over his face leaving the scene.

Around 7:30am the next morning, his houseman, Henry Peavey, found Taylor dead in his apartment.

Victim's Condition at a Glance:
A mysterious doctor from the crowd that had gathered in Taylor's home, pronounced the director dead by way of natural causes. The fact is that he never turned over the body before making his declaration. He was never heard from or identified after that point in time. It was also said that Paramount Studio executives were called to the scene before the police.

Taking a Closer Look:
Paramount studio instructed Taylor's houseman to clean up the scene of the crime as they seized all letters from the home. The police arrived on the scene after it had been compromised by the cleanup. Upon turning Taylor's body over they concluded that he died of a single gunshot wound to the chest.

Due to the presence of money on his person, a two-carat diamond ring on his finger, and other valuables in the room, the police decided it was not a case of robbery gone wrong. They instead ruled it a homicide by way of gunshot wound to the chest. As a result of the investigation several suspects were identified.

Defendants' Account of Events:
The last person to see the director alive was Mabel Normand. She was questioned in the investigation of Taylor's murder. Normand had asked Taylor for help with her cocaine addiction. With every relapse Taylor grew frustrated and agreed to help the police file charges against her drug suppliers. It was this reason that lead to the suspicion that her suppliers had gotten word of the news and decided to retaliate against the director. While the suspicion held, Normand was ruled out as a suspect.

The person who found Taylor's body was Henry Peavey. He had a criminal background and was arrested a mere three days before the murder. While the media believed he was the murderer, the police never indicated that he was in fact the murderer.

Edward Sands was Taylor's houseman before Peavey had taken over the position. Sands disappeared after the murder had occurred. Police believed he had a motive to commit the crime. Before his position was given to Peavey, Sands had wrecked the director's car and vandalized his home, for which he was later fired.

Another suspect was Charlotte Shelby. She had reason to harm the director due to his sexual relations with her daughter when she was aged 17-19. The police also found out that Shelby had owned a .38 caliber gun, which is the same caliber as the round found in Taylor's chest. Shelby ditched the gun and fled the country for a few years to avoid questioning by the police. Her other daughter later accused her of committing the murder during a heated argument.

The last suspect with some significance to the case was Margaret Gibson. The actress was said to have made a confession of guilt for the crime while on her deathbed in October of 1964.

Other persons of note in the case were Mary Miles Minter, the daughter of Charlotte Shelby, who had a crush on Taylor. It is unclear whether they were ever intimate. Also, Charles Eyton who was a producer with Paramount and one of the first to arrive at the home after the body was found. He discovered Taylor had been shot when he attempted to move the body. Finally, Faith Cole MacLean and her husband Douglas were Taylor's neighbors and saw a man lurking in the alley, heard a loud bang and then saw him leaving Taylor's home. They were not able to identify the man but remarked he seemed to have heavy makeup on his face. It was thought that the suspect could have been a female dressed up as a man.

Case Conclusion:

The murder of William Desmond Taylor is an unsolved mystery to this day. On her deathbed, Mary Miles Minter is said to have stated, "My mother killed everything I ever loved". (3) Although the suspect list runs long, the lack of evidence leaves no real indication of who the murderer was.

The Death of Thelma Todd

Date: December 16, 1935
Location: Pacific Palisades, chocolate colored 1934
Lincoln Phaeton
Victim: Thelma Todd
Suspect: Pat DiCicco, Roland West, Jewel Carmen, Lucky
Luciano, Alice Todd

Thelma Todd's backstory:
Thelma Todd was born, Thelma Alice Todd on July 29th,
1906 to parents John and Alice Todd of Lawrence,
Massachusetts. As a young girl, Thelma Todd was
excelling in academics and aspired to be a teacher. It was
during her teen years when she decided to go in another
direction with her career. At 19 a young Todd won the title
of Miss Massachusetts. The title opened up the door to
what was the start of her film career.

Todd played in only supporting roles during her career in
silent films. When the era of the Talkies came about, she
was given an opportunity to shine by producer Hal Roach.
In the early 1930's Todd was starring in feature films
alongside famous actors of the time. In 1931 she was
offered, and accepted, her own slapstick comedy series.
The star was coined *The Ice Cream Blonde* in Hollywood.

While the star made appearances in over 119 films, she
sought to get involved in other projects including opening a
trendy cafe in Pacific Palisades. Sidewalk Cafe, which she
had named the business, attracted the likes of some of
Hollywood's biggest names, as well as tourist and
Hollywood hopefuls. The last film Todd was to make was
titled *The Bohemian Girl*. After her death Roach re-shot the

film, and only allowed Todd to appear in one musical number.

On the Morning in Question:
The night before her death Todd had attended a party at the Café Trocadero. During the party she had gotten into an argument with her ex-husband but remained in good spirits for the remainder of the night.

On the morning of December 15th, 1935 ,her chauffeur drove her home from the party. Thelma Todd's body was found slumped over in the front seat of her chocolate colored 1934 Lincoln Phaeton, the car that had been parked inside of her garage.

Victim's Condition at a Glance:
An L.A. coroner ruled Todd's death as accidental at first glance. They noted that she had died from accidental carbon monoxide poisoning. The police originally concluded that Todd must have been trying to warm her car before leaving her house.

Taking a Closer Look:
During the investigation and Grand Jury investigation, it was discovered that Thelma was found with a broken nose, marks around her neck and a couple of cracked ribs. There were blood spots on her mouth and in her car. This discovery suggested foul play. Around the time of her death it was known that Todd and her ex-husband Pat DiCicco, a mobster and right hand man to Lucky Luciano himself, had a public argument in the days before the incident occurred. They were in the middle of a nasty divorce, as reports came out that DiCicco had been abusive to Todd in the past. Todd also had a previous

relationship with Luciano during which he beat her and provided her with amphetamines.

Todd's current beau was Roland West. They owned a restaurant in Malibu together with West's wife, Jewel Carmen, called Thelma Todd's Sidewalk Café and all lived together in the duplex above the restaurant. Todd's body was found in the garage. Carmen knew of West and Todd's relationship and didn't seem to mind until the restaurant started losing money and she blamed Todd. She was said to have threatened to kill Todd.

Finally, Todd's own mother and only heir, Alice Todd, was reported to have been bragging about building a giant mansion. It was not clear where she planned to get the money for such a huge expense.

It was said that the night before she died the star was in good spirits. Those closest to her made note that the actress showed no signs of unhappiness.

Taking it to Court:
The case was taken before a Grand Jury. No evidence was found that suggested she had been murdered. The group decided that the case be ruled an accident. Further investigation by the proper authorities was ordered.

Case Conclusion:
The case was again tried in court in front of a jury to see if there was a basis for an on-going investigation. The jury decided that the star died by accident with some suggestion of suicide and the case was ordered closed by the Homicide Bureau.

Scandals and Mysteries 1940-1980

Hollywood History 1940-1980

In the 40's, the world was struggling through World War II and the movies of the time helped get the public's support for the war. During the war, Hollywood tried to gain the support of local towns and the American People in general. After the War, the House of Representatives launched an investigation. The House believed that communist activities were behind the making of the films that were so well received by the public. The house did find some communist individuals who would become known as the Hollywood Ten. Identifying these individuals, who subsequently went to jail, lead to the establishment of the Blacklist in the 50's.

Around this time the film industry changed. As the number of televisions in the American home increased, the need to go to the movies and see a film decreased. People were staying in as opposed to going out. As a result Hollywood had to make a change, or go packing. Of course they chose the former and took risks to stay relevant in the 60's. Films began to hire younger employees and started to focus on films that included sex, violence, and humor in their story lines. This introduction started a new era in film history, alongside the new era came new talent in the business and more scandals.

The Bugsy Siegel Scandal
Date: June 20th, 1947
Location: Virginia Hill's Home, Beverly Hills, California
Victim: Bugsy Siegel
Suspect: Unknown
The Evidence: .30 caliber round found at the scene

Bugsy Siegel's Backstory:

Bugsy Siegel wasn't your typical Hollywood man. While he knew big names in the business he was a gangster from the start. Bugsy Siegel, named Benjamin Siegel was born February 28th, 1906 to Max Siegel and Jennie Riechenthal in Brooklyn, New York. His early life was described as meager. A young Bugsy and his parents struggled to survive in a home of seven.

Siegel dropped out of school as a young boy and took to the streets. He was determined to live a better life than his parents had. Bugsy began committing theft on the Lower Eastside of Manhattan. When he met up with Moe Sedway, his theft game turned into a protection racket. He forced shop owners to pay him for every pushcart. If they didn't pay up, he would burn their inventory.

Meyer Lansky later introduced Bugsy to the mob lifestyle. He was recruited as a bootlegger and hit man, and he handled business across many major cities. While in the bootlegging business he befriended known gangsters like Al Capone and even secured enough money to buy himself an apartment at the Waldorf-Astoria Hotel.

By January 1939, the young gangster was married to Esta Karkower who he had known from his childhood, though the marriage was short lived and the two split in 1946. In the 30's Siegel began engaging with top members of the mob like Lucky Luciano and Frank Costello.

After Siegel's tip to the IRS of Waxey Gordon's tax evasion, a hit was placed on him. He found the two that were supposed to be gunning for him and retaliated against them. After the subsequent murders of the two guns for hire, Bugsy gunned down their brother who had plans to expose Bugsy's crime syndicate.

After word got out about his attack on the brother Bugsy fled to California. When he was successful in Los Angeles, Bugsy set his sights on Hollywood where he was welcomed by the stars. Bugsy threw lavish parties in his Beverly Hills estate and even had relations with a few Hollywood actresses.

The Greenberg Murder:
A member of Bugsy's Murder Inc. group, Harry Greenburg, threatened to rat on the group and a hit was ordered on him. Bugsy, along with several other men were implicated in the murder. While awaiting trial Bugsy received preferential treatment. The trial pushed on, but after two witnesses were killed and no additional witnesses stood to take the stand Siegel was acquitted of all charges.

After the acquittal Bugsy set his sights on Las Vegas. He took over the Flamingo Casino and ran the business in an attempt to become a legitimate businessman, though it was said Siegel threatened the previous owner into signing over the property. During his reign as casino owner Bugsy not only put money into building up other casinos, he gave back to charitable organizations in the area.

On the Night in Question:

Bugsy and associates were at the home of Virginia Hill, a known mob associate and Bugsy's lover, in Beverly Hills. Virginia was not at home having had an argument with Siegel and flying off to Paris to cool down. At some point in the evening shots were fired into the window of the home hitting Siegel twice on the side of his head. One bullet entered his cheek and exited his neck. The other bullet hit his nose near his right eye socket, the pressure blowing his left eyeball out of its socket. Other bullets hit his lungs. The rounds fired were from a .30 caliber M1 carbine military grade rifle.

Victim's Condition at a Glance:

The L.A. Coroner assigned to the case noted the Cause of Death (COD) as cerebral hemorrhage. The death of Bugsy Siegel was ruled a homicide by way of gunshot wounds to the head.

Taking a Closer look:

The hit on Bugsy was rumored to have been a contracted agreement among the Board of Directors of the Syndicate. Though some of the attendees at the alleged meeting were said to disagree with the decision, a contract was put on Bugsy's head.

Case Conclusion:

No one was ever implicated in the murder of Bugsy Siegel. Following his death he was the basis for many movies that sought to depict his life on the big screen.

Frances Farmer's Backstory:

Frances Farmer was born Frances Elaine Farmer to Ernest Melvin and Cora Lillian Farmer on September 19th, 1913. Farmer was a success from the start. As a young girl she won her first award. She had written an essay titled "*God Dies*" based on her skepticism of religion and the existence of a higher power. The Scholastic Art & Writing Awards issued an award of $100 to her. Farmer held many jobs as a young girl. All the money she earned through her jobs went to pay for her university fees.

Farmer became a student at the University of Washington in 1935, where she went on to win a contest that awarded her the opportunity to visit the Soviet Union. It would be her chance to see the Moscow Art Theater and she welcomed the opportunity. On her way back to the University Farmer stopped in New York where she was offered a seven-year contract from Paramount Pictures. This started her film career.

Farmer left Washington and set out for Hollywood on her 22nd birthday. She starred in several films, and while her stardom had reached successful heights the actress was far from thrilled. In a time when movie execs governed your life, Farmer rebelled. She refused to attend Hollywood parties or even date actors in general. She did not want the limelight on her and in response she headed back to New York where she began her work on Broadway.

The star was cast in a play titled *Golden Boy* by the Group Theater. She helped the play receive rave reviews and success. After the group planned to tour the play in London, Farmer was removed from the cast. She set her sights back on Hollywood. She made a deal with Paramount Pictures to make movies three months out of the year, and the other months she would spend acting on Broadway. While she was making movies and gracing the Broadway stage Farmer had some troubles ahead.

Arrest:

Farmer had been arrested twice in her career. She was to become known in Hollywood as a woman with a bad temperament. In October of 1942 she was arrested and taken to jail, but later released and required to pay a $500 fine. In January of 1943 the actress was back at it. This time she was charged with the assault of her hairdresser. Farmer had dislocated the woman's jaw. It was said that upon both arrests Farmer had acted erratically, and even threw an inkwell at the judge on her second arrest, exclaiming she wished to have her attorney present. Her behavior was met with a stay at L.A. General's Psychiatric Ward.

Hospitalization:

After a stay at L.A. General, Farmer was transported to Kimball Sanitarium where she received a diagnosis of paranoid schizophrenia. After a brief stay Farmer began experiencing problems at the facility and walked away. She had been injected with liquid shock therapy. Farmer's mother won legal guardianship and moved her back home with the family to Seattle, Washington in 1943.

It was not long before Farmer and her mother began arguing and when Farmer attacked her mother she was sent to Western State Hospital. Three months after Farmer's commitment to the hospital she was released. While there she received electro-shock therapy. It was not until she had taken a trip with her father through Nevada in 1944 that Farmer had another episode that would lead her mother to recommend she go back to Western State Hospital.

Farmer would stay at Western State for five years before being released. Farmer noted the time as a very horrifying one. She wrote a book titled *Will There Be Morning* where she described her experience at the facility. She wrote that she was subjected to eating her own feces and was forced to engage in sexual acts with male staff members at the facility.

Case Conclusion:
Farmer died as a result of esophageal cancer in 1970. Her book became the driving force behind an advocacy group's push to abolish the practice of psychiatry. The actress left behind an outstanding career.

The Black Dahlia

Date: January 15th, 1947
Location: Los Angeles
Victim: Elizabeth Short
Suspect(s): Over 50 including Cleo Short, Robert Manly, Jack Wilson and Mark Henson
The Evidence: Packages to the press containing her items, several ligature marks on her body

Black Dahlia Backstory:

The Black Dahlia was born Elizabeth Short on July 29, 1924 to her parents Cleo Short and Phoebe Mae Sawyer. She was born in Boston, Massachusetts but grew up in a town called Medford. After losing the family's money in the stock market crash, her father disappeared. Short's mother moved the family into a small apartment. At 16 years old Short was sent to live with relatives in Miami.

When Short turned 19 she made her way to Vallejo, California to live with her father. Later Short moved to Santa Barbra where she was arrested and tried for underage drinking. Short was then sent back home to her mother. She ultimately ended up back in Florida where she accepted a proposal from an Air Force officer named Matthew Michael Gordon. He died in a plane crash and they never married.

In the months leading up to Short's death, she was broke and living anywhere she could. One of her roommates stated Short didn't have a job and boasted a new man on her arm every night of the week.

The Day in Question:

On January 15, 1947 Mrs. Betty Bersinger discovered Short's body. Her body had been cut into two pieces and was facing upward. Short's body was lying in the dirt and her hands were placed above her head. It was believed that Short's body had been cleaned before being discarded. No blood was visible and her intestines were neatly tucked away under her body. Short's face had also been slashed at the corners of her mouth, called the Glasgow Smile, and she had several contusions on other parts of her body.

The coroner reports noted that Short had ligature marks on several places of her body including her wrists and neck. He noted that the cause of death was a hemorrhage caused by the blows she sustained to her face and head. The media coined Short as the Black Dahlia. It was in relation to the dark colored suit she had been last seen in before the morning in question. It was reported that Short was unrecognizable at the scene. The LAPD had to send her fingerprints to the FBI who were able to identify her.

After the media sensationalized the case, a person claiming to be the murderer began sending items belonging to Short to the press. Several days after the murder occurred some of Short's personal items were found on top of a dumpster miles away from the crime scene.

Suspects:
Robert Manley: He was the last person known to see Short alive. He maintains that he picked her up on a San Diego street corner. As she was standing alone, he convinced her to let him give her a ride home. After she was asked to leave the home where she was staying,

Manley came back and picked her up. He took her to a local motel for the night and the next day drove her to Los Angeles. He left at 6:30pm to return home.

Cleo Short: Short's father lived three miles from the dumpsite. He maintained the pair hadn't talked for years and refused to identify her body.

Mark Henson: The package that was mailed to the media had one item that had Henson's name embossed on it which gave the police a reason to bring him in for questioning.

Jack Anderson Wilson: Wilson was suspected in the crime after giving details to a writer by the name of John Gilmore. Wilson, a drifter, made comments about the case that only a person closely linked with the crime would have known. Before any arrest or interrogations could be made, Wilson died in a fire.

Case Conclusion:
The police believed that someone she did not know attacked Short. Being known as a flirt, it may have been a male she picked that night.

Marilyn Monroe

Date: August 5th, 1962
Location: Marilyn Monroe's home
Victim: Marilyn Monroe
Suspect(s): Several, including Robert Kennedy
The Evidence: Multiple eyewitness statements, drugs found in her system

Marilyn Monroe's Backstory:

Monroe was born Norma Jean Mortenson in 1926 to parents Gladys Pearl Baker and supposed father Edward Mortensen. She was born in Los Angeles County Hospital. The early life of Monroe was a troubled one at best. Her mother suffered from mental instability and turned Monroe over to a foster home so she could be properly cared for. This was to be one of many stays at orphanages. At 16 a friend of the star proposed marriage in order to stop the continuous moving from home to home.

Her husband, a member of the Marines, was stationed in the Pacific and Monroe went to work at an aeronautical plant working on an assembly line. It was while working at the plant that she was discovered. A 1945 snapshot of the starlet working, turned into a successful modeling career and landed her in front of big named executives at 20th Century Fox. Monroe was asked to do a screen test for the studio, which she aced. The brunette changed her hair color to her iconic platinum blonde and changed her name to Marilyn Monroe.

She was offered a six-month contract with the studio. Her first appearances were as an extra, not the featured performer as she had hoped. It wasn't until 1947 when she got her first credited role. By the end 1947 the relationship between Monroe and 20th Century Fox had ended and Monroe retreated back to taking on more modeling jobs.

During one of her shoots she was introduced to talent scout Johnny Hyde. The meeting would later open up the door to a six-month contract with Columbia Pictures. Over the next several years the actress/model made several appearances in movies, which were dramatic and comedic roles. A deal was even worked out for Monroe that included a seven-year contract with 20th Century Fox.

Several years later, Monroe began experiencing health problems. She frequently reported having insomnia and visited a number of doctors. As she collected more and more drugs from the doctors she would visit, Monroe was becoming addicted. It was around this time when Monroe became difficult to work with on the set. Many of the people she worked with described the actress as unpredictable and demanding.

Start of Controversy:
Monroe met President John F. Kennedy in May of 1962, at an early birthday party for him. Reports state that Monroe, under direction from Kennedy's brother in law, sang Happy Birthday to him. It wouldn't be long before Monroe fell in love with Kennedy. Reports have long stated that Monroe would make frequent calls to the White House to speak with the President. She believed the two would marry once he left First Lady Jacqueline Kennedy.

There were reports that she called the White House and told Mrs. Kennedy of the affair to which Mrs. Kennedy replied, "Marilyn, you'll marry Jack, that's great... And you'll move into the White House and you'll assume the responsibilities of First Lady, and I'll move out and you'll have all the problems".(4) The affair ended sometime after the call. During Marilyn's final days it was reported that the President's brother, Robert Kennedy came to visit her.

On The Night in Question:
On Saturday August 4, 1962, after a typical day for Monroe, she seemed to be in good spirits. In the late afternoon, her friends recalled, Monroe began to act strangely seeming to be heavily under the influence. She made statements to friend Peter Lawford that he should tell the President goodbye and tell himself goodbye.

On the morning of August 5th Monroe's doctor reported her suicide to the police. When Sergeant Jack Clemmons arrived on the scene three people were present. Clemmons was led to Monroe's body. She was lying nude in bed with bottles of sedatives lying nearby. The scene appeared to be staged as Clemmons thought the body had been laid out carefully and noted that victims who overdose usually vomit and have convulsions and they die with their bodies contorted.

Clemmons took the statements of those who were first on the scene. They include Eunice Murray (Monroe's housekeeper), Dr. Ralph Greenson, (Monroe's personal psychiatrist) and Dr. Hyman Engleberg, (Monroe's personal physician). The trio noted that they had found the body hours earlier, but had contacted 20th Century Fox before calling the police. The initial coroner's report stated that the mixture of barbiturates found in Monroe's liver was the cause of an overdose and there were no findings that indicated foul play.

Case Conclusion:

While her death was ruleda suicide, the fact remains that there is some suspicion surrounding her death. On the night before she was found dead, her doctor reported he had given her a sedative when a friend became concerned about her well being. Another friend reported that Monroe had insisted she knew a secret about the Kennedys and apparently told another friend the shocking truth, before leaving the phone to investigate a disturbance at her front door.

It was later reported that a visitor who was in the home before Monroe's death, was asked to leave the home by Robert Kennedy and two other men. The guest maintains he left the home and when he came back the actress was lyingface down on her bed holding a phone.

Date: August 8th and 9th 1969
Location: Tate/Polanski and LaBianca homes
Victims: SharonTate and guests, Leno and Rosemary LaBianca
Suspect(s): Charles Manson and Associates

Charles Manson Backstory:
Charles Manson was born Charles Miles Maddox on November 1st 1934 to mother Kathleen Maddox, and presumed father Colonel Walker Scott. The earlier years of Manson's life proved to be shrouded in darkness. He had a mother who was said to rely heavily on beer and a father who was absent from his life. Manson reported that his mother had, allegedly, traded him for a pack of beer to a woman who was barren and longed for children. It was later reported that Manson's uncle found him a few days later.

It was some years later when Manson's mother and her brother were charged with robbing a service station and were sentenced to five years incarceration in 1939. Manson went to live with relatives. Upon his mother's early release, she set her sights on home, and went to get her son. The better life she had intended for him became frequent stays in run down hotels.

At age twelve Manson was sent to the Gibault School For Boys in Indiana. The boy only stayed ten months before running away. Over the next several years of Manson's life he was in and out of prison and youth detention facilities. During one stint in prison a young Manson reportedly told prison guards that he wanted to stay, telling them that he wasn't ready to go out to the real world because he had been locked up for so long.

Arrest:
Manson was first arrested at the age of 13. He and another boy were reportedly breaking into grocery stores and robbing them. The crimes led the youth to an Indianapolis juvenile detention facility where he maintained he was sexually abused. Broken down and just ready to go, Manson and a few companions broke out of the facility.

They did not get far as they were captured and charged with the federal offense of taking a stolen car across state lines. The crimes led Manson to D.C. National Training School for Boys. It was during his stint at the facility that he was deemed illiterate and said to have exhibited signs of aggressive antisocial behavior by his caseworker. In 1957 Manson was transferred to Natural Bridge Honor Camp. While at the camp, Manson sodomized a young boy that led him to be transferred to the Federal Reformatory.

In May of 1954 Manson was paroled from the Reformatory and went to live with his mother. At the time of his parole he met his future wife Rosaline Willis. It was only a short period of time before Manson was out committing crimes again. He was charged yet again with taking a stolen car across state lines. By September of 1958 Rosaline had fallen in love with another man and she and Manson started the divorce process.

Manson was paroled from prison again but returned after he violated conditions of his parole. He was sentenced to

McNeil Island Penitentiary. It was during his time here that he discovered his love of guitar.

After Manson's release from prison he met with Dennis Wilson, of the Beach Boys who in turn introduced him to a producer. The producer worked on the production of Manson's album. It was around this time that Manson began following the teachings of Scientology. He established a group of loyal followers called The Family.

In 1968 The Family moved to Spahn Ranch, which had previously been used as a set for western productions. The owner of the ranch allowed the group to live rent free in return for sexual favors. The women also acted as Seeing Eye guides for the man.

Turning Point for the Family:
1968 - The family gathers around a campfire where Manson discusses the social turmoil going on and the black rebellion. He maintained that the Beatles *White Album* directed the group and they had to save worthy people from the coming uprising.

1969 – January: The Family moves to Conoga Park to gear up for what they called Helter Skelter.

1969 – February: Manson gathers his final thoughts for an album he believed reflected the black uprising and annihilation of whites.

1969 – July: Manson decides the blacks need help getting Helter Skelter started and enlists a man by the name of Bernard 'Lotaspoppa' Crowe to gather funds. Crowe who had been duped by a member of The Family threatened

Manson and The Family. Manson did not take kindly to the threat and shot Bernard.

That same year, under the direction of Manson, The Family visited Gary Hinman who they believed had inherited a large sum of money. Hinman claimed he did not have any money and was held captive for three days before Manson showed up. Manson slashed Hinman's hand before ordering Family Member Bobby Beaussoleil to stab him to death. Before leaving the scene the words *Political Piggy*, with a Black Panther symbol, were drawn on the walls of Hinman's home in his blood.

1969 – August: It was August 6th when Beaussoleil was arrested for the crime, having been pulled over by the police in Hinman's stolen vehicle with the murder weapon in the car. That was the day that Manson declared Helter Skelter had arrived.

On the nights in question:
Late August 8th and Early August 9th Several Family members, under direction from Manson, went to the home of Sharon Tate. As they walked up the embankment they saw the headlights of a car coming toward them. A key member of The Family, Tex Watson, jumped in front of the vehicle and ordered the boy, Stephen Parent, to get out of the car. Parent begged for his life as he was stabbed with a knife and shot five times in the chest. The Family then pushed Parent's car further down the driveway, and made their way inside the Tate home.

Sharon Tate and Jay Sebring were ordered to the living room where they were brutally stabbed to death. Tate, who was two weeks away from giving birth, was shown no mercy. She was stabbed 18 times. The Family wrote "Pig" on the wall of her home in her blood. Two other guests, Abigail Folger and Voytek Frykowski were brutally murdered out on the lawn.

August 9th At 8:00 am the bodies at the Tate home were found by the housekeeper and the investigation into the murders began.

August 10th Around 1:30 am, not pleased with how sloppy the Tate murders had been, Manson tagged along with The Family members to ensure the job was done right this time. He led the group to the home of Leno and Rosemary LaBianca. Manson went inside the home and tied the occupants up. He ordered The Family to finish the job and returned to the Spahn Ranch. The LaBiancas were stabbed to death by a bayonet. The word "War" was written on the stomach of Mr. LaBianca, and the words "Rise" and "Death to Pigs" on the walls.

August 10th Around 8:30 pm, the LaBianca's son found their bodies as he returned home from a camping trip.

August 12th The police stormed Spahn Ranch, arresting Manson and 25 members of The Family in relation to an auto theft ring.

September '69 A month after the crimes a member of The Family that had been tried and convicted in the Hinman case, confessed to her cellmates.

December 1st, 1969 Police arrested the members of The Family who were suspected to be involved in the Tate and LaBianca murders.

Taking the case to court:

June 15th 1970 Members of The Family stood on trial for seven counts of murder and one count of conspiracy. Manson tried to represent himself in court, but as a result of his unprofessional erratic behavior, the right was revoked by the judge. On the first day of trials Manson was said to have a red x marked on his forehead. Prosecutors maintained that Helter Skelter was the reason behind the killings.

During the trial proceedings members of The Family had loitered around the entrances of the courtroom and appeared at trial with swastikas. During the trial several defendants did not take the stand. Manson, who took the stand, tried to avoid guilt saying that it was the music that had told the youth to rise up, not him.

January 25th Each of the defendants was found guilty by the jury. On April 19th, 1971 the judge sentenced all defendants, including Manson, to death.

Case Conclusion:

As a result of the trial and conviction of Manson and his followers a host of retaliation murders took place. This led to several more arrests and convictions. Let it also be noted that in 1972, as a result of California v. Anderson, those convicted in the Tate and LaBianca murders received reduced sentences. The abolishment of the death penalty made them eligible for life sentences

Scandals and Mysteries 1980-Present

Hollywood History 1980-Present

Even with a long history of scandal, Hollywood continued to grow. The 80's saw the birth of blockbuster movies and franchises such as the Star Wars films. Such changes came at the height of economic growth and technological advances. It was during this period that multiplex movie theatres came into existence. These changes had a positive impact on shaping Hollywood.

Video players and VHS tape also appeared and people were now able to take a movie home and watch it in comfort. The rise of movie rental stores like the popular Blockbuster only aided in the success of filmmaking.

In the 1990's the United States became heavily indebted to foreign countries. The economy had become vulnerable as the country's debt increased. The huge debt that we as a country owed created a decline in film production and jobs in general. Low-budget films had become the new norm in the industry. Industry workers sought out other opportunities as the work became less than desirable.

Workers often turned to work in the retail industry, taking on jobs that helped in the expansion of retail stores. In the 2000's the need for the studios to produce movies for the foreign market ended. The rise of new technologies such as computer generated graphics made movies more exciting to view.

Late into the 2000's the War in Iraq helped aid in the recession. It was the recession that caused people to spend less on luxuries. This made the film industry change the way they made films. They started going for simple plots that utilized special effects to draw in national and international viewers. Today the industry is still trying to recover from the hit they took from the recession, though powerful new technologies have made the film popular once again.

O.J. Simpson: The Death of his Leading Lady

Date: June 12th, 1994

Location: Outside Nicole Brown's condo

Victims: Nicole Brown & Ronald Goldman

Suspect: O.J. Simpson

The Evidence: Blood evidence, XL gloves, Footprints, Hair Evidence

O.J. Simpson Backstory:

While O.J. Simpson has gained a lot of media coverage in the past, talk of his life before fame is rare. The media insists on talking only about his adult life, which has been the subject of multiple controversies. O.J. Simpson was born Orenthal James Simpson to parents Jimmy Lee Simpson and Eunice Simpson, in San Francisco, 1947.

Simpson's childhood was average at best, though he did have to wear braces on his legs until he was five. This was due to the development of rickets. Simpson's parents separated and he grew up with limited means, living with his mother in the Potrero Hill Projects.

Living in the projects set Simpson on a path that would eventually lead him to a youth detention facility. After his brief stay in the facility, seeking to gain some structure, the youth played high school football at Galileo High School. Upon graduation Simpson played for a junior college in San Francisco, even earning the position of running back for the All-American Team.

From there Simpson moved on to become a running back for the University of Southern California. His success in football at the high school and collegiate level made way for him to be drafted by the Buffalo Bill's. After several seasons with the team, Simpson was traded to the 49ers. After his football career ended Simpson tried his hand at acting, even gaining several lucrative endorsement deals.

Simpson has been married twice, the first time in 1967 when he married longtime girlfriend Marguerite Whitley. The couple had three children before getting divorced in 1979. Simpson married Nicole Brown in 1985. They had two children.

The Controversy: The Night in Question-
On June 12, 1994 Nicole Brown and her friend Ronald Goldman were found dead outside of her condominium. Eyewitness reports state Simpson was seen wearing a dark colored sweat suit that night near Brown's home. After a loud thump was heard, people nearby reported seeing a man wearing clothes similar to Simpson's fleeing the scene.

Evidence Found at the Scene:
Evidence found at the scene of the crime made him a suspect in the case. Along with a pair of bloody gloves, there was hair evidence found on Goldman's shirt, and in the home, consistent with Simpson's DNA. The blood evidence found at the scene also matches Simpsons DNA and was found near bloody footprints. Blood was also found in Simpson's car and home. It was consistent with a cut on his hand that he stated he received from a broken glass on the plane home from Chicago upon hearing of his wife's death.

Court Proceedings:
Simpson was arrested in connection with the murders and subsequently charged with murder. A significant amount of

evidence implicated Simpson in the murders. Famous lawyer Johnnie Cochran had Simpson try on the bloody gloves, which did not fit. During Cochran's closing statement, he stated, "If it doesn't fit, you must acquit." (5) Though Simpson was found not guilty in the criminal case against him, he was found guilty in a later civil case and ordered to pay over $33 million in damages.

Case Conclusion:
After criminal proceedings ended Simpson wrote a book titled, *If I Did It: Confessions of a Killer*. The book was a confession of his crimes. The rights from the book were awarded to the Goldman family by a Florida bankruptcy court.

Bonnie Lee Bakley and the Trial of Robert Blake

Date: May 4, 2001
Location: Vitello's in Studio City, California
Victim: Bonnie Lee Bakley
Defendant: Robert Blake

Robert Blake Back Story:

Robert Blake was born Michael James Vincenzo Gubitosi. He was born to his parents Elizabeth Cafone and Giacomo Gubitosion September 18th 1933 in New Jersey. Blake's childhood was filled with abuse. It was said that his father often abused him as a young child, and he was also bullied in school. The tension in his home led to him run away at the age of 14.

He got his start on the big screen playing Tote in a movie called Bridal Suite. One of his more memorable roles was in the TV series *The Little Rascals*. After his appearances on the popular show, Blake made a series of appearances on other shows. During his adult years Blake joined the Army, eventually returned to film, and became a seasoned Hollywood actor.

It was in 1999 when Blake met Bonnie. Though she had a shoddy past with men, Blake married her. It was reported that the marriage came about when Bonnie became pregnant with the star's child.

On The Night in Question:

On May 4th, 2001 Blake took his wife Bonnie to dinner at Vaitello's Italian Restaurant. Before driving away from the restaurant, Blake left Bonnie in the car while he went back inside of the restaurant to retrieve his revolver. Moments later Blake returned to see his wife, Bonnie, slumped over in the front seat of the car. She had been shot to death.

Victim at a Glance:
The victim was bleeding from gunshot wounds sustained to her head.

Taking a Closer Look:
When the investigators took a closer look they found that the gun Blake went back in the restaurant to retrieve, did not match the one that fired the fatal shot to her head. Some believed that a lot of people had motive to kill her due to her past. Bonny was money hungry, and she was the type to get it by any means. Because of her criminal record and her track record, she was considered a professional lady of the night with a hit list.

Blake's Account of Events:
When leaving the Italian restaurant Blake realized he left his gun in the establishment. Going back to get it, he left his wife in the car. When he came back she was dying. He ran for help, but it was too late. Bonnie died soon after.

Taking it to Court:
On April 18, 2002, Blake was arrested, alongside his bodyguard, in connection with the murder. The arrest came about after a professional stuntman, Ronald Hamilton stepped forward. Hamilton told the police that he had earlier been approached by Blake to execute a hit on his wife. Later, another man came forward with a similar story. On April 22nd Blake was charged with one count of murder, a charge that included the possibility of the death penalty.

Blake pleaded not guilty to the charges against him and subsequently posted bail in the amount of $1.5 million dollars. In December of 2004 the case went to trial. The prosecutor maintained that Blake set the murder in motion to get out of his marriage. The defense's case centered on a lack of evidence.The jury went into deliberations on March 4th of that year. It wasn't until March 16th that they returned a verdict of not guilty.

Case Conclusion:
After the verdict, the Bakley children filled a civil suit against Blake, naming him liable for Bonnie's death. The jury returned a verdict of guilty and ordered Blake to pay $30 million to his children. The verdict left Blake on the verge of bankruptcy.

Anna Nicole Smith

Date: February 8th, 2007

Date: February 8th, 2007
Location: Seminole Hard Rock Hotel, Room 607
Victim: Anna Nicole Smith
Suspect: Howard K. Stern
The Evidence: Several legal drugs found in her system

Anna Nicole Backstory:

Anna Nicole Smith doesn't really need much of an introduction. The star was an acclaimed model, actress, and in her later years a TV personality. The Hollywood star is most noted for her appearances in Playboy. Her popularity as a Playmate pushed the actress into stardom. Anna Nicole Smith was born Vickie Lynn Hogan on November 28th 1967 in Texas. Her parents were Donald Hogan and Virgie Mae, of Texas. Upon the divorce of her parents, Anna was raised primarily by her mother, who remarried a few years later.

Anna dropped out of high school in the 10th grade because she was not doing well in school. It was around the age of 22 when she met her first husband Billy Wayne Smith. The two had a child together whom they named Daniel Smith. Two years later the couple separated. In 1991 Smith became a stripper, which she turned into a lucrative modeling career. Upon seeing an ad for Playboy, she set her sights on becoming a Playboy model. She ultimately succeeded in gracing Playboy's 1992 March issue. After her set in the popular men's magazine, Anna obtained an endorsement deal from Guess Jeans and Hennes & Mauritz.

Scandal of 1991:

In 1991 while working in a strip club, Smith met an oil tycoon by the name of Howard Marshal. Marshal was 89 and Smith was 26 years old at the time of their marriage. It was reported that Smith did not tend to traditional wifely duties. The two were reported to have never lived together during the marriage. It was a union brought on by Anna's love of money, at least that what her critics have said to the media. It was less than two years before Marshal died.

Upon the death of her husband, Smith was set to inherit his billion-dollar estate. Marshal's oldest son thwarted those plans. Several trials ensued over the matter and the results were as varied as the venues where they occurred. A California judge ordered Smith to collect more than $449,000,000 from the estate, while a Texas judge maintained she had no right to the inheritance. The case would later go before a federal court where her claims were rejected.

The Fall:
In the wake of her husband's death Smith had plenty of success but her life would take a turn for the worse following the death of her son Daniel Smith. In the wake of his death Smith was devastated. Reports claim that Smith even climbed inside her son's casket, wishing to be buried alongside him.

On the Night in Question:
Smith was found near death in her hotel room at the Hard Rock Hotel located in Hollywood Florida. Until the paramedics arrived on the scene, Smith's bodyguard administered CPR. Upon arrival to Memorial Regional Hospital, Smith was pronounced dead.

Victim at a Glance:

The medical examiner ruled that the cause of death in the case was combined drug intoxication. Though no illegal drugs were located in her system, the mixture of medicines she had taken proved deadly. Her death was ruled a suicide.

Taking the Case to Court:

Several of the prescription drugs found in Smith's system were prescribed to her friend Howard K. Stern. There have been reports surfacing that indicate Stern may have played a role in the star's death. An L.A. judge was said to have convicted Stern on two counts of conspiracy in relation to her death. The charges were in reference to Stern's obtaining prescriptions under false pretenses and giving them to Smith, which aided in her death. As of now, Stern could face 3 years prison time at sentencing.

Chris Benoit: House of Horror

Date: Saturday June 23rd, 2007
Time: 3:30p.m.
Location: Atlanta, GA
Victims: Chris Benoit, Daniel Benoit, and Nancy Benoit
Suspect: Chris Benoit

Chris Benoit Backstory:

Chris Benoit was born on May 21st, 1967 in Montreal, Canada to Michael Benoit and Margaret Benoit. His parents and others around him maintained that as a teen Benoit was driven. His idol had long been identified as a wrestler named Dynamite, who Benoit met at the age of 15. It was at this point that he determined he was going to break into the wrestling industry and become a star. By 18 Benoit was a wrestler at the amateur level. He began training with Stu Hart, a wrestling pro. His father backed the star through his every move, often encouraging him in various ways.

After training under Hart, Benoit went pro in 1985. He got his start in what was known as the Stampede Wrestling promotion. His debut match was in November of 1985 in a match against Calgary, Alberta. He was placed on a team of wrestlers and later went on to defeat his opponent. The victory won him the first of several titles. When the Stampede closed its doors Benoit moved to the Japanese wrestling circuit on the recommendation of a friend.

Upon entering the Japanese circuit Benoit begin to train to improve his skills. It wasn't until after months of strenuous physical activities that he made his debut. He debuted in 1986 under his real name. Three years later he added a mask to his stage costume and donned the name The

Pegasus. He went on to win his first title in the circuit in 1990. He lost it a mere three months later in a match against Jushin Liger. In 1992 Benoit broke into World Championship Wrestling (WCW) with fellow Canadian wrestlers.

Benoit made his debut on World Wrestling Entertainment, Inc. (WWE) in 2000. He debuted with three other wrestlers as a team named The Radicalz. A few months after their debut in the WWE the group won their first championship title. It was during his time with WWE that a rivalry between Chris Jericho and Benoit developed. They ultimately teamed up and won several matches together before Beniot suffered a neck injury that would take him out of the game for an entire season.

Family and Marriage:
Benoit married twice and had three children. Benoit divorced his first wife around 1997 before marrying Nancy Sullivan in 2000. After just three years of marriage Nancy filed for divorce. She cited cruel treatment as the cause of the breakdown of their marriage. She later retracted the filing.

On the Night in Question:
Benoit was scheduled to appear at a WWE event the night of the murders. Friend and fellow wrestler, Chavo Guerrero, called to check on him when he failed to show. Benoit spoke with him briefly on the phone stating he had missed his flight due to his wife and child being sick. He stated that the two were suffering from food poisoning. He told WWE executives that he had to accompany his wife to the hospital after she began to vomit excessively, but maintained that he would make arrangements to fly out the

following morning

Friends of the family began to worry about the couple and called the Fayette County police, who subsequently conducted a welfare check on the couple. On Friday, June 22nd, the police entered the home and discovered the bodies of Nancy, Chris, and Daniel Benoit.

Nancy at a Glance:
Her husband strangled Nancy to death. Injuries sustained to her back indicated that Benoit used the force of his knee to press into her back to provide leverage for the strangulation. A towel was wrapped around her body, and blood was underneath her head.

Daniel at a Glance:
The child was found in his room. Benoit had suffocated him. The coroner's report indicated that the drug Xanax was in the child's system.The presence of the drug indicates that the child was sedated before suffocation.

Chris Benoit:
After murdering his wife and son, Benoit hung himself. He laid Bibles next to the bodies of his family.

Responding to the Crime:
After reports surfaced about the crime the media went into frenzy. Many people painted a monstrous picture of Benoit. But friends of his say that he loved his family with all his heart, and don't know what could lead him to commit such a horrific act. Some people believe that his motives were in relation to testosterone injections he had been taking. Others noted it might have been a result of injuries he had sustained from wrestling. His father, along with a doctors'

study on Benoit's brain, said the action could have been caused by brain damage.

Michael Jackson: The Death of a Legend

Date: June 25th, 2009
Location: Jackson's home in Holmby, California
Victim: Michael Jackson
Suspect: Dr. Conrad Murray
The Evidence: Propofol in his system

Michael Jackson Backstory:
Michael Joseph Jackson was born on August 29th 1958, to his parents Katherine Scruse and Joseph Jackson. Jackson's early life in Gary, Indiana was a turbulent one. The family lived in a three-bedroom home with 12 occupants. His father was allegedly abusive to all of the Jackson children, and his mother was a devoted Jehovah's Witness.

Jackson has credited much of his success to his strict upbringing. However, public opinion maintains that his childhood was the source of the many controversies Jackson experienced in his adult life. Jackson's first success came as a member of The Jackson Five. The group, composed of Michael and his brothers, became a part of Motown Records and traveled on tour throughout the Midwest.

Jackson ventured off into his solo career after the Jackson Five's record sales began to decline. Jackson had much success winning several awards, including a Grammy and a Billboard Award. From then on the star produced several successful recordings such as "Thriller", "Billie Jean" and "We Are The World."

Start of Controversy:
Jackson's Skin: Growing up, Jackson had a medium

brown skin tone. As he grew in popularity his skin color changed. At the height of his career Jackson's skin was much lighter. Many thought the star had bleached his skin, but it was later revealed that he had a skin condition called Vitiligo.

Neverland Ranch: Jackson purchased a $17 million dollar ranch that he called Neverland. The property included a host of carnival rides, a security staff, and movie theater.

Sexual Abuse: Reportedly, Jackson frequently invited young children to his home. A 13-year-old boy reported the first allegation of sexual abuse in 1993. The father of the child maintained there had been abuse in an attempt to ruin Jackson's career and obtain money from the star. The singer didn't pay up, and the charges were subsequently dropped.

That same year police stormed Jackson's estate, and recovered a book that contained numerous pictures of unclothed boys. A second investigation began in 2003 headed by the Santa Barbara Attorney's Office. The investigation was in response to a television broadcast that featured the pop icon holding the hand of a young boy. Jackson was acquitted for all nine counts against him.

Berlin Incident: In 2002 Jackson was televised dangling his young child over the balcony railing of his hotel. He was heavily criticized in the media for the incident.

The Day in Question:
On January 25, 2009, Jackson's personal physician, Conrad Murray, went to Jackson's room and found him with a very light pulse and not breathing. 911 was called at

12:21 pm. Attempts to resuscitate Jackson by Murray and the paramedics who arrived on the scene three minutes after the call took place were ineffective. Jackson died of cardiac arrest in his home, located in Holmby Hills, Los Angeles, California.

The Scandal: Jackson's cause of death was listed a lethal mixture of drugs in his system. Two days after Jackson's death, Conrad Murray, Jackson's doctor reports that Jackson had been given injections of Propofol. He maintained that the drug was administered to the star to help him sleep and they were in the process of weaning him off of the drug.

Case Conclusion:
Dr. Conrad Murray was charged and found guilty on November 7, 2011 of involuntary manslaughter in the Jackson case. Murray was sentenced to four years in prison.

In Conclusion

From its early days as a one-hut town to the apex of today's movie industry, Hollywood has made its mark on the world. It has made stars out of the misfits of society, and sensationalized scandals. From its inception to now, Hollywood continues to shine. Through the hunger and thirst of hopefuls wanting to blossom in the industry, through scandal and murder, Hollywood will push on.

References

1.www.brainyquote.com/quotes/authors/m/marilyn_monroe
_7.html

2.www.brainyquote.com/quotes/authors/j/jack_nicholson.ht
ml

3.http://www.crimelibrary.com/notorious_murders/celebrity/
william_d_taylor2/14.html

4.*These Few Precious Days: The Final Year of Jack with
Jackie*, author Christopher Andersen

5.www.brainyquote.com/quotes/authors/j/johnnie_cochran.
html

Dear Readers,

I want to thank you for purchasing my book. I hope you enjoyed reading about the scandals and murders in this book as much as I did researching them. If you enjoyed this book please share it with family and friends.

Thank you for your support.

Sincerely,

Mike Riley

Please be sure to check out my other book,

More Hollywood Murders and Scandals: Tinsel Town After Dark Volume 2.